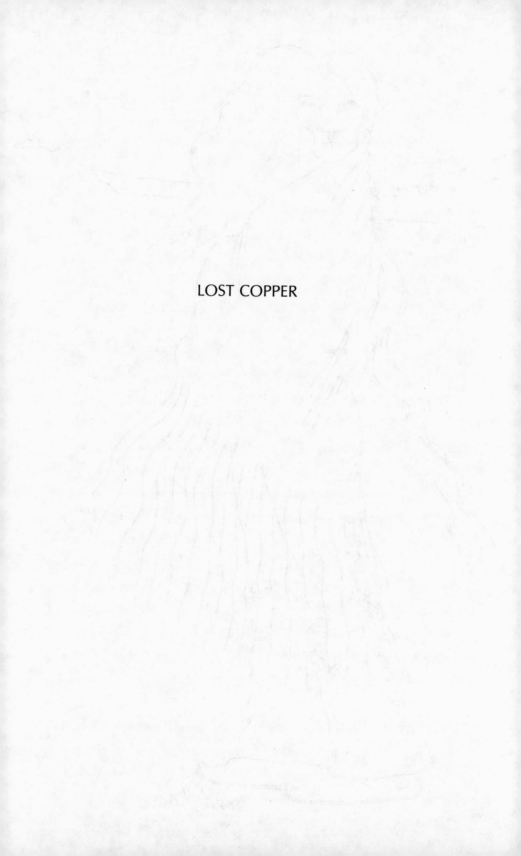

LOST COPPER

LOST COPPER

poems by
WENDY ROSE

Illustrated by the author

With an introduction by
N. Scott Momaday

1980
MALKI MUSEUM PRESS
Banning, California

Library of Congress Catalog Number: 80-81849
Printed in the United States of America

DEDICATION

HEADS UP!
This one's for
  Arthur Murata
  Terry Garey
  Maurice Kenny

The author wishes to express deep appreciation to the editors and publishers of the following chapbooks, anthologies, and journals, in which some of these poems have appeared:

A Journal

Akwesasne Notes

Academic Squaw: Reports to the World from the Ivory Tower (Blue Cloud Press)

Before Columbus Catalog

Beloit Poetry Journal

Beyond Rice

Builder Kachina (Blue Cloud Press)

La Confluencia

Contact II

Contemporary California Women Poets

Contra Costa Advocate

Dodeca

Early American

Greenfield Review

I Am the Fire of Time

In Her Own Image: The Lives and Work of Women Artists

Journal of California Anthropology

KPFA Folio (Pacifica Foundation)

Long Division: A Tribal History (Strawberry Press)

Mango

The Native Perspective

Networks

The Next World
New World Press Collective Anthology of
    Women Poets
Phantasm
Pocket Poetry Reprint Series
Poetry of the American Indian (American Visual
    Communications Bank)
Reaping
The Remembered Earth
River Styx
Room
Shantih
Sibyl-Child
Strata
Sun Tracks
The Third Woman
This Song Remembers
Time to Greez: Incantations from the Third World
Trends (Paisley, Scotland)
Waters

   Publication of this book was made possible in part by
a grant from the National Endowment for the Arts.

PREFACE

The good, strong things which constitute this book are numerous and diverse. Wendy Rose reaches into many corners of experience, and her perceptions are acute and trustworthy. Indeed, diversity may be the key word here, for LOST COPPER is not a collection that one can characterize easily. Easy labels will not do. Here, for example, is certainly a literature of protest, but to say that is to mislead, for protest is not the essential vitality in this instance. Here is a celebration of the earth, to be sure, but neither is this the central fact. Time is involved here—this work involves time; time involves this work—not as a subject particularly, but as a dimension in which myriad subjects exist in crucial relation to each other. But even time is not the heart of this matter. I have come to believe that the syllables and words and verbal patterns of LOST COPPER refer immediately to spirit. And the spirit of this book is nearly ineffable. It is an abstraction that inheres in the concrete world, like the hawk's shadow that glides upon the canyon wall. It is elusive. One cannot be sure what it is, and one cannot doubt *that* it is. It is supremely native.

Nor is this a book of "Native American" literature, in any narrow sense. One does not read very far into it before he understands that the writer moves from one frame of reference to another with remarkable facility. The voices of LOST COPPER proceed from very different realizations—ethnic, philosophical, professional.

But the native voice is pre-eminent in this case. In order to appreciate the range and power of the singer's voice, one must appreciate the nature of the song. LOST COPPER is not made up of poems, I think, but of songs. This seems to me an important distinction. The rhythms here are not those of traditional English verse. The images are of a different order, too. The language—the old language of Donne and Shakespeare and Pope and Hardy, after all—is put to a different use. It is brought to bear upon a *native* sensibility, a *native* landscape, a *native* experience. It is made a close reflection of American Indian oral tradition, a tradition of song and prayer and story, rather than of

poetry as such. It is older than literature, older than
writing. It is as old as language itself:

> We map our lives this way: trace our lineage
> by the corn, find our words in the flute,
> touch the shapes that feed us with dry seed.
> We grow as shrines grow from human belief;
> we sing a penetration through our pottery bodies.
> Nothing is old
> about us yet;
> we are
> still waiting.

It ought to be borne in mind that Wendy Rose is a
painter, a maker of paintings as well as a maker of songs.
The two disciplines require different creative processes.
Writing is necessarily abstract, symbolic, cerebral. The
creative information of painting on the other hand is concrete, spontaneous, emotional. Wendy Rose brings these
disparities into balance. The lines above, from "Walking
on the prayerstick," constitute a remarkable equation in
this respect. They cast the shadows of language upon the
substances of the earth, as it were. Time and language are
concentrated in corn and the flute. Human history is con-
tained in dry seeds and the earthen vessels that our bodies
are. We are indeed waiting.

> I think I need an Indian star
> for mixing colors I was born to paint;
>
> the ties of earth distract my glands yet
> were they gone
>
> I would drift nameless
> a simple idea to carve from fire,
> a new sky that loves red / white.

The "ties of earth"—and the spirit they engender—are the
vitals of this book, and the book is a celebration.

N. Scott Momaday

San Francisco
2 January 1980

CONTENTS

Frontispoem: Lost Copper

Time to tend the fields again
where I laid my bone-handled spade to earth
and dug from its dirt the shy childsongs
that made my mouth a Hopi volcano.
My hands retreat dusty and brown
there being no water pure enough
to slide the ages and stones from my skin,
there being no voice strong enough
to vibrate the skin and muscle apart.
Like a summer-nude horse I roll on my back
and fishtail my hips from side to side;
then on my belly, my navel gone home,
I scrape my cheek and teeth and ride.
From there I rise of earth and wind
to the height of one woman
and cup my breast to the hollow-gourd vine
to feed the place that has sent me songs
to grow from the ground that bears me:
this then my harvest

squash-brown daughters,
blue corn pollen,
lost copper.

PART ONE

PROTECTING THE BURIAL GROUNDS

"It would be better for the
Indians to become human slaves
than to remain free animals."
—Spanish explorer, 1590

". . . you tell people where a site
is, and they start to dig it . . . and
the only thing they are looking
for . . . is arrowheads and beads.
And some people like to collect
skulls . . ." —Archaeologist, 1972

"For sale: American Indian skull,
guaranteed authentic. Good con-
dition, $300 or best offer . . ."
—published ad, 1976

To some few Hopi ancestors

No longer the drifting
and falling of wind
your songs have changed;
they have become
thin willow whispers
that take us by the ankle
and tangle us up
with red mesa stone,
that keep us turned
to the round sky,
that follow us down
to Winslow, to Sherman,
to Oakland, to all the spokes
that have left earth's middle.
You have engraved yourself
with holy signs, encased yourself
in pumice, hammered on my bones
till you could no longer hear
the howl of the missions
slipping screams through
your silence, dropping dreams
from your wings.
                    Is this why
                    you made me
                    sing and weep
                    for you?

Like butterflies
made to grow another way
this woman is chiseled
on the face of your world.
The badger-claw of her father
shows slightly in the stone
burrowed from her sight,
facing west from home.

Winslow: A town near the Hopi reservation in Arizona.

Sherman: A Bureau of Indian Affairs school in Riverside, California, to which many Hopi were forcibly sent.

Oakland: A major "relocation center" for Indians during the 1950's.

Walking on the prayerstick

When we go to the fields
we always sing; we walk
each of us at different times
on the world held
like a feathered and fetished prayerstick.
We map our lives this way: trace our lineage
by the corn, find our words in the flute,
touch the shapes that feed us with dry seed.
We grow as shrines grow from human belief;
we sing a penetration through our pottery bodies.
Nothing is old
about us yet;
we are
still waiting.

Imagine you float
to those white scar marks
on the granite where water
drains breaking open the rocks
below, turning to ice
and raining on in.
This is where
we first learned to sing
on ancient mornings
because our skin was
red sand, because our eyes
floated in flashflood water,
because our pain was made
of burdens bound in cornhusk,
because our joy flowed
over the land,
because touching ourselves
we touched everything.

The small circling bird: Milpitas

Four summers on her shoulders
little Indian girl
with ravenish whirly hair;
little Indian girl
49 in her eyes
dancing to the thundery friends
in her daddy's drum.

Seeking sound
like a trail in the wind
she round-dances, rabbit-dances,
war-dances, throws out
her tee-shirted left wing,
wordlessly circles the singers
and touches each one
with a long flight feather,
circles the singers
counter-sunwise,
walking on stars.

She makes rainbows
about her ankles
and with them guards
what's hers:
nine singing men
at the Drum and
her daddy.

49: Type of contemporary Indian song, meaningful to the
   People, but associated with having fun rather than anything
   solemn.
Drum: In this case referring to a pow-wow drum. A group of
   men sit in a circle around a large drum, each one with his
   own drumstick, singing. The poem takes place before the
   pow-wow begins, when people are arriving and warming
   up

The well-intentioned question

Here you are
asking me again
what is my Indian name

and this was the time
I promised myself
I'd tell the truth

and stand hard
and smooth
as madrone,

tight as mesquite
answering you.
My Indian name soars

in pinyon-wood flutes,
stopped at one end
by asphalt; my Indian name

catapults
like condors gliding inland
on the power of prayer;

my Indian name bumps
on the backs
of obsidian-hard women

sighting me with eyes
Coyote gave them;
my Indian name howls

around the black hats
of fullblood men
on Friday-night search

for fairness or failing that
for fullness;
my Indian name listens

for footsteps
stopping short of my door
then leaving forever.

Southern-stepping the Slow Dance

Thirty now
but fifty tomorrow; the days
are recorded
by a silent drum.

Something I see inside myself
makes the years skip & scuttle
quick as skipping-stones
that tap the water
as they fly by.

Southern-stepping: A pow-wow dance style performed by
    women.

The urban child listens

Like in another time
sticks crack in a smokey open fire,
my voice whistles in and out
of the children like a native wind.
How could I know
they would need to learn it all
from the beginning
how the corn-tassels light up
like sheep-fat candles,
how they become metallic threads
of silver spider web, how the wind
is dusted down and sweet
as it bears the rain on its back,
how thunderheads bunch and clench
like fists working in the sky
to soften the earth?

My throat is the distant noise of traffic,
of city streets, has taken the shape
of buildings, of avenues, of control,
of garden flowers wet with insecticide,
of steam and stark horizons.
Never good at keeping secrets
I whisper how Coyote speeds
through our lives anyway
looking for his gambled shells
though we might have missed the sight
of canyons filling with sand-bubbling water,
might have missed the breath held
as the thunderheads swelled.

Long division: A tribal history

Our skin loosely lies
across grass borders;
stones loading up
are loaded down with placement sticks,
a great tearing
and appearance of holes.
We are bought and divided
into clay pots; we die
on granite scaffolding
on the shape of the Sierras
and lie down with lips open
thrusting songs on the world.
Who are we and do we
still live? The doctor,
asleep, says no.
So outside of eternity
we struggle until our blood
has spread off our bodies
and frayed the sunset edges.
It's our blood that gives you
those southwestern skies.
Year after year we give,
harpooned with hope, only to fall
bouncing through the canyons,
our songs decreasing
with distance.
I suckle coyotes
and grieve.

Protecting the burial grounds

Womb-stolen woman, round woman:
the sad earth-stained leaves
that swallow your buckeye burden
are sterile in grinding-hole bedrock,
waylaid into deep-sea galaxy of obsidian.

Ohlone Woman, Costanoan Woman:
with saltwater I see you
cupping the coast live oak,
waking up the soaproot shoots
to line your chin
with tattooed puberty,
a woman's badge
that from village to village
shadows your soul
with a thirst for names.

Abalone woman, obsidian woman:
it's you that's spawned
by grasshopper hands.
I am fat and honored
before you.

Tattoo: It was the custom among most California Indian groups
to tattoo a young woman's chin when she reached puberty.

Vanishing point: Urban Indian

It is I in the cities, in the bars,
in the dustless reaches of cold eyes
who vanishes, who leans underbalanced

into nothing; it is I
without learning, I without song
who dies & cries the death-time,

who blows from place to place on creosote dust,
dying over & over. It is I who had to search
& turn the stones, half-dead crawl

through the bones, let tears dissolve in dry caves
where womens' ghosts roll piki
& insects move to keep this world alive.

It is I who hold the generous bowl
that flows over with shell & stone
& buries its future in blood, that places its shape

within rockwall carvings. It is I who die
bearing cracked turquoise & making noise
so as to protect your fragile immortality

O Medicine Ones.

Red wood: Some of our roots in China

The remotest days
of our growth in China
are sweeping by my throat;
in that ancient song
I heard the sherds
of frost-white Grandmother
peeling the red bark back
along the tall trees,
deftly skinning the forest
with her eyes that are black stars
through which we see each other
as we dance. Huffing, leaning
on right-angled sticks,
the weight is placed forward,
our knees are bent; we touch and twine
like that knee to knee,
our feathers swinging back and forth
as parts of the animals we are.
Our feet powder the painted hill dust
and raise valley fogs of blue and yellow
as we stretch and turn our toes
lifting acorns up from the earth.
Giving these now back to the trees
we rain on them and rain on them
to leach the taste of lightning
from their souls til they are ready
to be swallowed as mush.
Being with her voice one moment
Owl, then Antelope, then Bear,
then Hornet: Grandmother's guessed
in the handgame a good guess again
and her pink granite hands
scoop up all the shells.

Handgame: A guessing game played throughout the west by
    Indian people. A great deal of gambling occurs, and a tour-
    nament may go on nonstop for several days.

I expected my skin and my blood to ripen

"When the blizzard subsided four days later [after
the Wounded Knee Massacre], a burial party was
sent to Wounded Knee. A long trench was dug.
Many of the bodies were stripped by whites who
went out in order to get the Ghost Shirts and
other accoutrements the Indians wore . . . the
frozen bodies were thrown into the trench stiff
and naked . . . only a handful of items remain in
private hands . . . exposure to snow has stiffened
the leggings and moccasins, and all the objects
show the effects of age and long use . . . [Items
are pictured for sale that were gathered at the site
of the massacre:] Moccasins at $140, hide scraper
at $350, buckskin shirt at $1200, woman's leggings at $275, bone breastplate at $1000."
—Kenneth Canfield, *1977 Plains Indian Art
Auction Catalog*

I expected my skin
and my blood to ripen
not be ripped from my bones;
like fallen fruit
I am peeled, tasted, discarded.
My seeds open
and have no future.
Now there has been no past.
My own body gave up the beads,
my own hands gave the babies away
to be strung on bayonets,
to be counted one by one
like rosary-stones and then
tossed to the side of life
as if the pain of their birthing
had never been.
My feet were frozen to the leather,
pried apart, left behind – bits of flesh
on the moccasins, bits of paper deerhide
on the bones. My back was stripped of its cover,
its quilling intact; it was torn,
was taken away. My leggings were taken
like in a rape and shriveled
to the size of stick figures
like they had never felt the push

of my strong woman's body
walking in the hills.
It was my own baby
whose cradleboard I held –
would've put her in my mouth like a snake
if I could, would've turned her
into a bush or rock if there'd been magic enough
to work such changes. Not enough magic
to stop the bullets, not enough magic
to stop the scientists, not enough magic
to stop the money. Now our ghosts dance
a new dance, pushing from their hearts
a new song.

Archaeology: How she was born

On May 7th my birth slid
along the innards of earth,
at cornplanting time circled
the longbones, tapped and left
the crusty-toothed skulls.

Today's prayers
are scented and brushed
with acorn, with buckeye,
with sweetgrass, with maize
and as they breathe
their last love-look on my body
they stretch themselves
guided by moon, to the place
where we sat down to gamble.

The bones clacked
under the game blanket
as we sang down the sun
in two teams of six.

Prophecy

This is the spring
I awaited through the cold,
from flowing grandmothers
with wedding belts wrapped tight,
finding days that still go on
with ritual and laughter,
never spending the night
bitter in thirst.
This is the spring
I awaited through the cold
my fingers grown tight
from holding bells meant for dancing,
turtle shells for my pounding feet,
my voice grown over with moss.

These are what is sung
as gold-skinned victory
for half-breed children
who know that flowers
are colored with tomorrow
yet are too brave for this life
or too exhausted.

Power of prayer

Singing & rattling the same words
over & over, leaving my throat
like white moths, these words
are addressed to a spirit grandmother
somewhere in the light that I see
from this high desert cave.

And the words come back, circle above me,
make me stop the song, drop the rattle.
In the sky or on sacred mountains
are there spirits who smile & murmur
"Grand Daughter"?

Buckeye

Buckeye endures on this land
where oak and screwbean bend
blackened into human hands.

Other native bones
swell into mountains,
run red with the story
of their Christian death;

other native tongues
drop in the sand
thick with Spanish,
trilling with hymns.

Survivor
Singer
Feeder
Doctor

Buckeye endures on this land.

Buckeye: A tree that provided a staple food for many California
Indian people; it was a deadly poison until it went through
a complex leaching process.

My red antennae receiving: Vermont

Here, too, the skin has been red
and the hands have frozen into wolverine feet
that bend into a welcoming gesture
through a distance that echoes in death.

Mountain to mountain (none of them so thin
as I know them in the west)
sound is cupped in the earth
to erupt in another time
when memory begins to edge away.

The voices have no end.
They are not stilled.
Songs steam
dipping into snow
as they look for familiar trails

for tracks left behind
by ancient tongues,
forgotten women and the places
they propped their burden baskets.

It may be confusion
or it may be anger
that slides native color
from these frozen cliffs
to harden in the cold air
midway between the source
and its hungry mouth.

Landscape for this Indian woman

I think I need an Indian Star
for mixing colors I was born to paint;

the ties of earth distract my glands yet
were they gone

I would drift nameless –
a simple idea to carve from fire,
a new sky that loves red/white.

On Indian Star I'll plant disks of garden,
concentric rows of air for corn

unbegun from seeds;
I'll place Outcast Kachina Woman to watch them

and lovingly touch
the petroglyphs on my bones.

Petroglyphs: Rock carvings.

The anthropology convention

From the day we are born
there are eyes all around
to watch our stumblings,
our contacts with the skin
of each other wrist to wrist.
When we pull in the world
about our bellies there are those eyes
watching for exotic pots of words
spilled from our coral and rawhide tongues.

O we are
the Natives.

Only the sounds of silence read our souls
like so many juniper essays; the reverse snap
of a leaf at thirty below, the jump
from tree to tree covered in squirrel-fur,
the bending round of snow-topped cactus
so tired, so tired. This planet
leaf with bent edges beginning to turn color
holds us up and binds us
to chromosome-licked bones.
And some part of this world
old and pagan as the ticks on my skin
just holds on.

For the White poets who would be Indian

For the White poets
who would be Indian

just once
just long enough
to snap up the words
fish-hooked from
our tongues.
You think of us now
when you kneel
on the earth,
turn holy
in a temporary tourism
of our souls.

With words
you paint your faces,
chew your doeskin,
touch breast to tree
as if sharing a mother
were all it takes,
could bring
instant and primal
knowledge.
You think of us only
when your voice
wants for roots,
when you have sat back
on your heels and
become
primitive.

You finish your poem
and go back.

Incident at a hamburger stand: Iowa City

My eyes so soon after sleeping
and without coffee until this moment
stick quick together,
the lids grinding and half open.

Already
the shoulders of a construction worker
square and solidify to remind me
"Girl, you are in the midwest now,
keep your place – eyes down
while I get a good look
at your fat Indian body
before I go" and then he turned

and said to his friends
"I'll wait outside
where it's not so crowded"
this last while turning his mouth
to where I was sitting
and pointing with his toothpick.

As he said
I kept my head down
hating myself for doing it;
beaded ear-rings
good southwest peyote rope
blasted along
the red of my cheeks.
One last swallow of creamed coffee
and I tip my head back
to defy him, square up my own shoulders
and refuse this white man's burden.

I am not angry you know
but wonder: what kind of man
can be like that
so early in the morning?

Peyote rope: A style of beadwork.

24

The red / white blues: Bicentennial poem

Never so strong
as to fly unassisted
I have left so much pain
on this world that
it seems to heave over,
no longer blooming its trees,
lambing its ewes,
elongating crystal.
What once was leaf
twisted from the plaster
is bloodless. I know
of passing for the unreal,
I know
of bloodlessness.

The solid creekwater
shapes a chrysalis
for its children
into which they will back
without human doubts,
without wondering
if flesh is real or
if what lies under
can die. I would burrow with them

had I my father's badger claw,
my mother's buckeye burden basket.
But the poisons in my soul
are not to be leached
with water. I lose count
slowly and out of step
of those elements
that pad me with mud.

Three Thousand Dollar Death Song

"Nineteen American Indian skel-
etons from Nevada . . . valued at
$3000 . . ."—Museum invoice,
1975

Is it in cold hard cash? the kind
that dusts the insides of mens' pockets
lying silver-polished surface along the cloth.
Or in bills? papering the wallets of they
who thread the night with dark words. Or
checks? paper promises weighing the same
as words spoken once on the other side
of the grown grass and dammed rivers
of history. However it goes, it goes.
Through my body it goes
assessing each nerve, running its edges
along my arteries, planning ahead
for whose hands will rip me
into pieces of dusty red paper,
whose hands will smooth or smatter me
into traces of rubble. Invoiced now,
it's official how our bones are valued
that stretch out pointing to sunrise
or are flexed into one last foetal bend,
that are removed and tossed about,
catalogued, numbered with black ink
on newly-white foreheads.
As we were formed to the white soldier's voice,
so we explode under white students' hands.
Death is a long trail of days
in our fleshless prison.

From this distant point we watch our bones
auctioned with our careful beadwork.
our quilled medicine bundles, even the bridles
of our shot-down horses.   You: who have
priced us, you who have removed us: at what cost?
What price the pits where our bones share
a single bit of memory, how one century
turns our dead into specimens, our history
into dust, our survivors into clowns.

Our memory might be catching, you know;
picture the mortars, the arrowheads, the labrets
shaking off their labels like bears
suddenly awake to find the seasons have ended
while they slept. Watch them touch each other,
measure reality, march out the museum door!
Watch as they lift their faces
and smell about for us; watch our bones rise
to meet them and mount the horses once again!
The cost, then, will be paid
for our sweetgrass-smelling having-been
in clam shell beads and steatite,
dentalia and woodpecker scalp, turquoise
and copper, blood and oil, coal
and uranium, children, a universe
of stolen things.

PART TWO

ACADEMIC SQUAW: REPORTS TO
THE WORLD FROM THE IVORY TOWER

"[Tucson Indian School's] . . . students are only one jump removed from the sagebrush and the witch-doctor, one generation removed from Indians who still walk barefoot and live the catch-as-catch-can existence of their ancestors . . ."
            —Randolph Shelton, 1950

"Indian children are beautiful and very lovable. They are also a genuine challenge to the teacher since they have more learning to do than most children . . ."
—Bureau of Indian Affairs brochure for teachers, 1977

"Don't expect to get special treatment in this department just because you're Indian . . ."
            —Anthropology professor, 1978

Academic squaw

Like bone in outer space
this brain leans to a fierce break;
with crooked muscles and names mis-said
we ethno-data heroically bend
further and further, becoming born
from someone else's belly.
When I wake before the sun and be still
I can feel the bone shape itself into words,
bone that is frame for Hopi blood
and hides its secret parts under
woven wool folds, lies with sheepdung
and stones and sheetmetal and sherds
to cover fragile thin places left
from the potter's fire.
The design was smudged, the bowl-rim warped,
from the beginning. The clay twists
in and around my jumping blood,
becoming the way those ancestors were –
anonymous native water sliding
from their throats
that left their track on me
but let me need to learn it
in a foreign tongue, look for its repaired form
in museums where the eyes are melted
out of the skulls yet manage
to peer from the mud lazy-stitched
to some random soul.
They give me, stretched across the desert,
their ethnography. I am being trained,
as the bones and clay bowls left open
are drained. Grandmother,
we've been framed.

Squaw: In modern usage, a derogatory term. It should be
        understood here in an ironic sense. I would not seriously
        call myself or any other Indian woman a squaw.

Unstoppable: Academic poets' cocktail party, Berkeley

> ". . . the literary history of the nation [America]
> began when the first settler from abroad of sen-
> sitive mind paused in his adventure long
> enough to feel that he was under a different
> sky, breathing new air, and that a New World
> was all before him with only his strength and
> Providence for guides . . ."   —Spiller, *Literary
> History of the World*

Unstoppable, anyway
out of place . . . won't sink
til winter.
I insist on my peekings
and flow whenever
the snow
turns its face.
I shout the desert
into the Arctic, showing up
like a bit of lichen,
a dry red spread on Mars
or something
equally incoherent.
I won't go down
in being unreal;
I won't go down
in being unheard.

Matriculation

1st Year

Sassed my way
through college.
The sounds
of a dozen generations
of grandmothers
were jangled
in their faces
by myself like
a mad eagle.
They really got mad
when I picked up the books
and like laundry began
to shake them clean.

2nd Year

The rattles and groans
of the speeches you give
might in another time have been
the wood and rope of tallships
sailing before the wind,
sent from golden thrones
for more and more gold.
You discover me
again and again.
Take my bones back with you
to prove the world is shaped
like a hen's egg, young
and untried, virgin
but older than you can know.

3rd Year

Pacing back and forth,
ignoring your blond-wood lectern,
you talk. We don't give history a fair shake,
        maybe there are ways that "race"
        makes you crazy or nonliterate
        or unlikely to invent the wheel.
Denying your belief in all that
you criticize the controversy
as you rip out the hocus-pocus answer
from my innards. Tying up my tongue
you grant me a new level graciously
of scientific integrity. But this
is something new.
You don't
see me.

4th Year

I test your speech like pottery,
ping my finger against it
and listen for the fragile hollow sound
that will hang in the air tightly
for a moment or two.
Your spaces, your intervals,
your unfilled ticked-carefully-off seconds,
are shapeless and opaque to me.
Your clock speaks in riddles.
You are strong only
where you are blown
forming glass into
twisted intersections
complex, weak, old,
breaking gently
on my trowel-ticked bones.

Dancing with the New Kachina: Worm Song

"It's time we stopped studying human society from the
level of tribal primitives. That's the worm's-eye view. It's
time to turn our attention as anthropologists to our own
civilization . . ."—Anthropologist at Berkeley, 1977

Is there a Kachina
for people like me
whose songs are too late
to be kiva-whipped,
too wild yet
to be PhD'd?
Metate-ground,
this semi-squaw listens
to how she's
out of fashion now,
how her turquoise melts
in the mouth of the city,
how her bones crack
like old excavated things,
how it is true
that her life is dried up
like its dances torn
by the arms of crumbling priests
in their ancient kivas.
I hear it.
The laughter of tourists mingles
with that of professors in my sleep.
It was a joke.
It was a fad.
Now the fad is over
and like a one-night stand in Gallup
we disappear over the fence
discreetly.

Kiva-whipped: A kiva is an underground chamber used, among
other things, for ceremonies. Whipping refers to a ritual that
occurs when a young person has reached the age of initia-
tion into the Kachina Society, of which all Hopi are expected to become members. Sort of like a Bar Mitzvah.

Metate: Flat stone upon which grain is ground.

Gallup: Reservation town in New Mexico, famous for native
"casualties."

Chasing the paper-shamans

Here I go drawing pictures again.
I illustrate a different world
as I chase the shamans who watch each day
to soak up the forming-eyes they had left
to be tended by me and be chased
onto paper. As I flatten them
their blood coagulates into legends of moss,
stories that split open in the shining stones
and the white peeled tamarack bark.

Within my skin Grandmother goes on laughing
and her eyes turn into distant black moons.
Her cells, handed down as surely as songs,
weave shapes as if tracing arroyos only to
color them with the airborne scent of sage.
I believe in them,
these hard-lined flat people
who are given life under my hand.
They are finished
as they direct the nervous spirit
on whose narrow back I ride.

Handprints

In this university
I am a red ghost
touching handprints
that gleam, bleached,
while like a witch
this Breed searches
for dark reflections
to spin from white spoor.
There is somewhere
a woman
built from earthen blocks
who is not
specimen,
sideshow evidence
for "affirmative
action".

With light and dark colors
the chancellor's necklace
is beaded on my loom;
it's the middle colors
missing, as my hands
are forced
into chiaroscuro designs.
It's a good word we say
when we meet, those professors
and I. Politely,
like civilized people,
they consider should they say
"good morning" or "how"
or keep silent, pretending
if they look the other way

I'll fade covered with blood
back to Wounded Knee, silently creep
into Lovelock Cave, wash up
on Alcatraz, or print my face,
crystallized by a camera,
into another closed history book.

Chiaroscuro: Designs formed from the contrast of black and
    white.
Lovelock Cave: A cave, once inhabited by very ancient people,
    in Nevada.

How I came to be a graduate student

It was when my songs became quiet.
No one was threatened,
no eyes kept locked on my red hands
to see if they would steal
the beads and silver from museum shelves.
When I became, in the owl's way, a hunter
they trusted the microscope
that hid me in the grass, that bent up
and over me too big to drive away.
That's how they knew
they could move in.

Those quiet songs
I could tell you
simply expose the stone spirit
of Warrior Kachina stepping sideways
through the village; or I could say
that the brave and ragged meat of me
is being tongued away by a foreign god.
I am shut away in a house
where all are dead and when it looks
like I may break loose they tell me
I'm *moving* now and congratulations . . .
all the time my stone-spirit song
grows and erupts and laps over the world;
my legs roll away like water on stone
going downhill to an ancient matrix,
uprooting in the spring and moving on.
It's that kind of moving:
from grave to grave.

Indian anthropologist: Overhanging
sand dune story

> "There is no more thrilling aspect for the an-
> thropologist than that of being the first white
> man to visit a particular native community . . ."
> —Claude Levi-Strauss, 1955

> "Don't let them ruin you like they've ruined
> some other Indian women I know . . ."
> —Sioux graduate student, 1978

They hope, the professors,
to keep the keyhole blocked
where my mind is pipelined
to my soul; they block it
with the shovel and pick
of the pioneer spirit,
the very energy that made
this western earth turn over
and throw us from her back
bucking and hollering like
stars were whipping her.
Mama Earth is wearing
her long-tongued mask of drought,
rolling and moaning
to smother the red-hot infants out.
And I feel it like a shiver,
like the sop of wet cloth
on red skin.
Parts of my soul come again and again
to face north, moss-covered,
to tap their names on my eyes,
to give me a pinch of tobacco,
to say I can go on like this
only if I shut my ears
but keep wide awake in the eyes.

Literary luncheon: Iowa City

According to the windows
that face the slow-spilling brown river
we are sipping not our coffee
but blizzard winds that surprise us
rolling in from the north.
Still-bare trees
are slowly colored white
and the earth implies
this is the source
of the cold I feel. Not so.

The great ones gather
at the university buffet
like cattle around
their alfalfa and barley.
I maintain
without willing it
an Indian invisibility.

Looking Back from the Mud

I must look fine as I stomp & stride
through the salt-marsh university halls.
That long-ago theme of "Indian power!"
is an old echo now; at the university
we pretend we are deaf.
After all, we're *in* now –
forget that steep burro trail
we climbed from the canyons,
forget that shoulder-deep snow
we pulled ourselves through,
forget the war rubble
through which we staggered
in the city.

Red hands that prodded new words into my mouth
have let me go alone into the furnace
drenched in native gasoline,
on fire with the fury
of disintegrating drums.
I look back from the mud,
erase the tracks behind me.

Was it all "to be somebody",
to "know the enemy", to be a "Skin, man"
urban kin to the ones at home?
Not one seed
has sprouted from my sweat.
Not one prophet
has thundered from my books.

"They gave all that expensive equipment
to the Indians . . . course the damn fools
just broke it . . ."   We damn fools.
We make cat's cradles of words
we write papers and stand at podiums
while they plot murder behind us.
All the words, all the ideas,
are equipment for fools to break.

At last
the rain has come.
The land & the redwoods,
the great fields of barley,
the citrus groves
begin to relax. The lakes fill,
the mudflats flood.
Earth
barren so long
conceives.

But I am not planting.
I am not praying.
I am not going slow with my planting stick
nor steady as I drop my pumpkin seeds.
I am not a patient woman,
I am not one to laugh at midnight
& pretend the ghosts
have not arrived.
I will not sing in the beautiful rain
as I have done so many years alone.
Living in this tunnel
I have learned to expect nothing.

With the knobs & dials
of fragile equipment
I'll slash my throat;
I'll hang myself;
I will throw my body down
from fluorescent lights
to bloody the computers
into reality.
I'll go out in the graves dancing!
I'll go out in the desert dancing!
I'll go out in the sky dancing!
I'll go out of this world
in a sheepskin casket
but I'll be dancing
the oldest dance I know!

PART THREE

LEARNING TO UNDERSTAND DARKNESS

"Ain't got no home in this
world . . ."—American
folksong

The requirements of a target

that you are still,
that you strike a pose and hold it.
You wait for each bullet
like different birds and cherish
how they push into your flesh.
You love the skill
that spaces your cells
so they are surrounded by pain
and you refrain from falling
but lift each limb, salute,
and let your life burst
from out of your soul
and only then at the
very end do you die.
Encore,
encore.

Learning to understand darkness

Night has drawn its knees up
near me and settled in, singing its slow
and mysterious songs, keeping itself black.

Night must be threatened some
to shrink like that and fold itself so
into a cold ball that drops to touch earth.

I hear the dawn before I see it
and begin to understand with respect that
dark form crouching and covering itself

with the sound
of a thousand insects.

The day I was conceived

was, they told me, the middle
of a yellow and turquoise time.
My Badger-father bent
his silver head to earth,

pulled at his finger till
they hardened, turned
to tufa. Then split the stone
and carved within

the marks of lizards, human hands,
Spider Woman, kachin-mana,
and the most ordinary of stones.
He poured next the moon,

molten silver, into creases
made ready. Like claws his fingers
held the stone made to plow and scrape
up through the world.

Badger-man, Good Hands, with blinded soul,
with an underworld glow,
was it a long time it took
to cool the tufa down, to split it,

solid-spilling moondust now marked
by billions of scars?
Mid-morning the heat began
and grew as a kiln but before that

a feather-mite of tufa lifted,
was set down and struck in the west
by acorn-tongues, cedar lodges,
touched by shells still wet

from the sea, carried away
in the mouths of dust devils.
He would need a bone medicine tube
incised with magic or obsidian

to see what he buried that day
to forget among the turquoise chips.
And so my origin is one
of rocks and badgers; I sing

but do not carve. My origin is one
of moondust and medicine;
I dance but do not pray.
My origin is one of maize and mesquite;

I grow but do not live.

Kachin-mana: Female Kachina, spiritual or holy being.
Tufa: Stone used in sandcasting silver.
Badger: Refers to membership in the Badger Clan.

The endangered roots of a person

I remember lying awake
in a Phoenix motel. Like that
I remember coming apart accidentally
like an isolated hunk of campfire soot
cornered by time into a cave.
I live even now
in an archaeological way.

    Becoming strong on this earth is a lesson
    in not floating, in becoming less transparent,
    in becoming an animal shape against the sky.

We were born
to lose our eyes in the Sun Dance
and send out lengths of fishline
for the clouds, reel them in
and smooth away all the droughts
of the world.

    Sometimes Medicine People shake their hands
    over you and it is this: to drop your bones
    into the sand, to view yourself
    bursting through the city
    like a brown flashflood.
    The healing of the roots
    is that thunderhead-reeling:
    they change and pale
    but they are not in danger now.

That same morning
I went for coffee down the street
and held it, blowing dreams
through the steam, watching silver words
bead up on my skin. The Hand-trembler said
I belong here. I fit in this world
as the red porcelain mug
merges in the heat with my hand.

On some future dig
they'll find me like this
uncovered where I knelt
piecing together the flesh
that was scattered in the mesa wind
at my twisted-twin birth.

Losing eyes in Sun Dance: Sometimes Sun Dance initiates would
stare at the sun.

Hand-trembler: A type of Medicine Person who diagnoses
what's wrong with you, in a trance-state during which the
hands tremble uncontrollably.

Twisted-twin birth: Some people were supposed to be born
twins; but instead they were united just before birth through
metaphysical means, and born as one individual. I am not
really one of these, but I use the *feeling* as a persona.

Portsmouth Square, Chinatown, San Francisco

Enough like a reservation
to not be foreign; old men
with nowhere to have been,
young women with nowhere to be.
We float under the sycamore trees
like premature blossoms in winter fog.
We do not suspect
that leaves will replace
this barren way
that we are.

I watched the old men play Go
many afternoons. Though I danced
through the middle of their dreams
they did not see me. We look through
a lens that is yellow and red:
images leak in and out, reflections vanish
in waves of colored light and reappear
as if the glass moved

but it's only our scorched history
smoking in the wind. Points are scored.
The thin leaves drop and are gathered up.
I am thin-leaving, expecting to return,
expecting to grow old.

Tennessee blackbirds

Having forgotten to secure permission
to live here I am applying one final time
for life. How I got this far I don't remember,
remember only how the pain was sharp
in every footfall along the way.
They're saying on the news

how Tennessee farmers will spray the blackbirds
till the oil is gone that keeps them from freezing,
that insulates them from the colorless plains
of Tennessee winter; and for each blue-black feather
dried to its death there I am stripped of my words,

dropped from my shadow, exposed
to the faceless devils in eastern snow
with only poems wrapped like Pendleton blankets,
my sticklegs bent and broken
and stuck in the ice.
Flight dissolves this spirit's last dream
of how it is to be frozen in life then

dissected while mute. One too many for earth
we Tennessee blackbirds are doomed from the nest
to drop in the pools, the puddles,
the drowning black grass.

Poems mark the seasons

I have chosen to take home
these leaves

for like words on a page
they are unyielding and stiff.
Widowed like the ice of spring
my hands are milked of words
so that all my paper rings fall off
as fingers are peeled
down to bone and cold dominates
all of my self.

I have chosen to sit at the stiffened edge
of autumn

and watch how the seagulls
fly into the sun to help it dip down
to its depth. I'll listen
to all the ways I can be alone
as only bones can be alone. The Hopi say
alone one is dead and one is dead
alone.

Detective work

Found the songs first
in little pieces
under a stone. Took all my strength
to gently roll the stone
and prod them out

but behind the yellow piss-pine
crouched the trickster, waiting
to put a mountain there.

Part of me lives in the library

Sunburnt, the skin
reddens in the womb;
ancestors skip stones
across the top of my heart
and boil me away from my soul.
Whirling down into space
I feel tied
to a woman's birth,
handcuffed and glued
to the rumble
of thirty years on earth.
I remember learning
to hide my bleeding nerves,
and scratch my name on pinyon
so no one would forget
this is the earth I touched.
And I beat myself till I cried
going to battle again and again
forever the burglar,
never the clanswoman.

I keep a careful watch
on the dreams,
through the pitch-sticky songs
as they return.
The landscape is wrong
but it's all there is.
Constellations and clocks
are not related to my eyes;
as they appear I sleep.

I was lifted from my mother
by the force of her feeling,
emerged in the smell of hate
displaced and weeping,
whirling the flush of magic
over my head.
Nightly the shadows flicker
and stick on me to be shed
like old hairs that blind me
in their tumbling.
How do the warriors say it?
   * It's a good day to die! *
Every day good enough,
every day a good death.
Blindfold
offered by Ogre Kachina;
fist of parched corn
from my father.

Potsherds

Leave   in the convent stillness of my shadow
enough of your having-been to cradle my love still inclined

toward fall, its borders dry having seen its dust tongued
and its full-day ripeness spread between your feet.

You should be dead. How you stiffen in my thoughts
and draw from my eyes opaque vision.

How simply you lean on the earth, its corporate strength
containing your weight. My fruit is in your conflict,

my quarrel with the clock's breath. My fear streams
into a bucket with foamy buffalo milk and that blood

is the joy swirled in. I hold tightly to songs
with steel fear knowing you will go

as the wild grasses go.

Poet's business: We Catholics
learned to love martyrs

Reach in deep
then leave me
to find the words
alone.
This world
is a pile of words
compost words
mountain-thick
words like bellows
squeezing and shaking
reason
into the same calabash
with pain.
Every moan
is a separate pulse,
a cause
for applause,
a line of shadows
struggling to be art,
sounds in a basket
bilingual and raw
in their singing.

Tricked.
Let me not touch the pen.
Let my voice be stilled under water.
Let anesthesia ride each nerve to the finish
and let the poet dissolve.
Let the bones melt into the rain
and disappear; let me disappear
and let those soft bones go.

Apology and flight

Against my own arm
this Miwok bone: might imagine
drying up in the ground
grey stump left
from clamshell ceremonies
so long ago as to never see
the inside of the missions
or be "reduced" or converted
or whipped for singing songs
to bring the salmon home.

On the eastern slope of Tamalpais
your strength was a legend;
on her breast as she slept
in the stormy summer air
you twisted the mussels from agate rocks
and pried them apart with your teeth.
At the edge of the bay
you placed rocks in the fire
and carried them to the temescals,
sprinkled them with water,
steamed the songs from your throat
and called the acorns
down from the trees
with the drip of your sweat.

I would not have you in my home
but here you are;
I would not bring you
from the sandy shell midden
but here you are;
I would not unbend you
from your final flex
but here you are;
I would not take you
from your moist recess
but here you are
and yet it was I found by you
where the backhoe scraped you
into this world

where I heard you calling from the field
and stopped at the sound of my soul
named in Miwok.

I hope you know I prayed
picking you up, this bit
of your slim arm bone.
I nearly hid you in my mouth
from the Sausalito eyes.

I prayed you would not see
what they'd done:
the houseboats on the bay,
the mansions on the hill,
the villages
flattened by Franciscan swords.
And I prayed
you would wrap a power
of spirit stuff about my hands
and plait my skin like a shrine
around you for we need such a weapon,
a bow of ghosts, or all of us will be
longbones upended and broken,
skulls disconnected from the earth,
teeth scattered like seeds
and frozen in the salt.

What's left of you, this:
of bone a single bit,
of blood a city on sand
that shook you into tomorrow,
the machinery of spirits
that wedged you between my fingers,
ancestors that trail me
through Sacramento
leaving ochre-stained bones
in the courtrooms.

Temescal: Sweat lodge.
Midden: Soil containing refuse and artifacts in an archaeological
    site.

The poet as unclaimed corpse

I have picked my bones before you,
autopsied my soul, filed
report after report to your bureau
on how death came carried by words
in weakening meter, in the false welcome
of parentheses, in the open mouth
of another dead poets' anthology.
A tiny view from my eye
shows grey-white feet
vapored into hell as if poets
never lived at all
but let their songs carry them
through life a bit unborn, a bit misty.

The name-tag on my toe
was written in disappearing ink.
Or was it just a number, a thumbprint,
tracks in the sand or snow,
some small sign that I lived
a life that was only half-done.
I have lived therefore desert-dry,
salty beyond absorption, and cold.
The steel against my backside now
is not so cold as all the ghosts
that fanned past my face
when I called to my friends.

I began as a song or an agony,
a buzz from the mother of tongues;
I end like that, laid out in diagrams,
to be buried in a strange land.

Montana

Ice
is a persistent gentle thing
creator whose voice
and northern shoulders
are burdened
with antler.

Autumn 1949
I might have waited like this:
bent into a bone cup
and trying to pull air about myself,
become acquainted
with the sharp breath
of a deadly red snow
that would
stain my skin.

I was tattooed by the ice
a signal that I sit alone
with songs hobbling my hands.

I was nearly one year old
and much farther west.

Voyage on the beads of her black rosary

A barnacle snaps
in its conical shell,
the smell of the wharf
a blanket: I back
into my infancy,
careful to keep my eyes
to the sea. The first bridge
is made of rosary beads;
I shake the dust
from each hailmary,
from the silver cross
and its tortured body.

It will be a Gothic cathedral
or painted adobe or grove of redwoods
where I kneel to remember
the nine tongues of my childhood.

Sister Lydia spoke
with a speech made of blades,
smelling and looking like moss,
feeling like dried shamrocks;
framed always
in black and white.
She fingered the wooden beads at her belt
and thought of the rosary
as weapon, as garotte. Strings
of round bruises rise on my soul
like blue marbles.

And the points they scored in clothing:
nylons, garterbelts, lipstick,
training bras, delicate gold rings
with amethyst stones, and white oxfords
on bloody socks from uphill climbs.

Where was that outdoor shrine – Tucson? –
where the Virgin moved as I knelt?
There was the pointing hand, the Spanish finger,
the lightning sizzling from her tongue;
she called me bruja, hermana de la noche,
and something else
that sounded like thunder.

That was the end of my praying.
My song stopped, struck in mid-air;
a quick flip back to earth
to steam like acid
in the votive candle rack.

Bruja: Spanish for "witch."
Hermana de la noche: Spanish for "sister of the night."

Indian 39,000 feet up

Below me
the boulders
are ticking
like time bombs.
Finally
a review
of this year:
a bend
in the backbone,
a break
in the rib,
a buckle
of the knee.

There's plenty of time
to run home now
if the steps are paced
consistently apart,
the route
well-planned.

Poem for September suicide: Euthanasia

Inch by inch
I lose my rainbow;
no one offers
to restore it.
You see how short
are thoughts like these,
clipped and caged
they tighten their grip,
page by page
they weep.
There is a dying woman
deep inside me,
beating her fists
on my inner skin.
She is tragic,
she is varicolored
with calico-printed hands
white-knuckled on my veins.
She is beautiful.
She could be Indian
or she could be White;
she could not
be doubted
for she is dying.
She offered her skin
to the last sea-storm
to blow over Berkeley
and was blown about
til the pieces fit.
The wind died down,
she came
rolling apart
this dying one,
this one whose dreams
were never enough
to make the water,
the seed, the soil
fit together.

Aging into death: Petrify then dissolve

Chinatown changes little
on the surface but inside ourselves
we feel the ancient arteries
crack.

Between levels of my skin
hard and grey we grow old together;
our cells learn in the neon flash
to shoot firecracker-swift
through the harbor city mug.
Like white moths in electric light
we are actors who read our lines
dangerously by surrounding
and ingesting the bay.

These words are camouflaged,
gotten loose; but I catch them again
as they bend and beat their edges
to fit the streets. Instantly
we are the great old sounds
that crash and crackle along Grant,
that like me are semi-legal,
unstoppable, grown too old
to be startled by noise or silence.

I go deathwalking to deeper waters,
to anonymous asleep fisher-fleets
that would never notice one more
silver bobbing sliver of meat
in their next evening's catch.
Like that I visualize my words
ending in the sea as food,
with gills stuck open and scales
attached by single threads. And the vision
is swept inside like a new scent,
something fresh, something still ahead.

These words must be remembered
as butchered things, as bits of life
thrown down; my hands remain living
only to catch the words up again,
silver fish that I must keep catching
and hauling onto my feet.

Trickster

Trickster's time
is not clicked off neatly
on round dials nor shadowed
in shifty digits;
he counts his changes slowly
and is not accurate.
He lives in his own mess of words,
his own burnt stew; he sees
when the singers are spread
and trapped by their songs,
numbed by the sounds of space
and reach their limit
so they can't hear the frozen music
circle above us like ravens or
like grubs flow into fleshy thrums
at their feet.

Trickster turns to wind,
Trickster turns to sand,
Trickster leaves you groping,
Trickster swings walking off
          with your singer's tongue
          left inaudible,
Trickster dashes under cars
          on the highway and leaves
          the crushed coyote,
Trickster bounces off whistling
          with his borrowed coat of patches
          and upside-down kachina mask,
Trickster licks stolen soup from his face
          and counts the slaps
          that hover in the silence
          near the place where
          they missed his face.
We see only his grey tail
bird-disguised
like a moving target
as he steals all the words
we ever thought
we knew.

What falls from the airplane

Words
that struggle
toward memory
potentially
ancient
as they sharpen
on snow-piled plains
far below;

these southern hills
are razor strap and talc
to the changes
in my voice.

I imagine
songs flying out
like fingernail parings
to enter tornadoes
through Oklahoma
in a fast 49:

I was almost with you –
all you Southern Drummers
– but settled for dipping my wings
silently over this land
cut by canyons
that keep us home.

PART FOUR

FOUR POEMS ESPECIALLY
FOR RON TANAKA

"The night which is closing in
takes possession of the centaur's
neck, his limbs; he is twisted and
tortured . . . his forthcoming
death benumbs him little by little
. . . he is superb in pride and
despair."—Unknown source,
                    from a letter

Netsuke

Deer
with fog antlers
angling in song,
your quiet song
ascends the sun.
You
gentle netsuke man,

you bring gods
from mere mortality,
you bring from the curves
of this earth

the shapes of songs
that high and clear
have kept hands warm
for a thousand years.

The golden noon of you
touches the red tears of me,
you let it turn
to silt, you
wash it
away.

Netsuke: Japanese artifacts, something like watchfobs, that are
counterweights to little boxes *(inro)* worn in the belt.
Netsuke and *inro* both tend to be intricately carved, often
beautifully simple. They are most often made of ivory, but
sometimes of wood, bone, or mother-of-pearl.

A return to pinpoints

He labors

his love a birth labor,
his songs long rope
that pulls stars about
to where they weep
unmolested
by astronomers.

Tanaka Tanaka
like the best Hopi silver
your soul is a secret
inlaid so deep
it takes having known
ancient caves
to see it.
Some of us come in

to sight along the edge
and fall, softly absorbed
by your bones. In our sleep
we are layered with your pain.
How you sing
those old mountain songs.

When you told me what they'd done:
Prose poem letter

Dear Ron
It was not easy for a young Indian woman
just starting out on her mountain hunts
to understand that assassins
are everywhere. I thought it enough
that your words had power
to locate my native soul lost in fog,
that your voice could home me in
like a crippled jet on a dark night.
I will not forget the exhibit of you
reading your work: slowly pacing
the width of the room, each step
the hesitation and halt of an ancient dance.
And from your hand there grew
a Japanese fan that tapped or opened
or took the place of fingers and fist,
that was not a gimmick for I know
that the slats of the fan were tendons
of your hand. Each mile of your pacing
stopped another heart among us
as you sang and murmured, water over stone,
a tumble of flute and drum and bamboo clacker.

And so it was not easy
to hear of you hanging by your tongue,
to understand that you had been beaten
by hatchet-poets with billyclub lines
and brass-knuckled rhymes.
They kept you sighted in their crosshairs
all these years I guess, waiting
for the moment you would release your power,
waiting for the secrets to leak
from your knees. As you locked away
the paper and pens that transform
your soul into shining pages
I shared each torture device with you
and the tightening noose as well. Among our own people
we still are not free, we still
must plant and pick and hide.

I am not alone. Because they heard you
there are co-conspiratorial stones
that have lifted from their mines and shone
that have been covered by the dark mud
of anonymity. And together we weep with you.
Just three things more, then we will go.
First, above all things you are a poet.
Second, like the buried netsuke
your strength is inside-out like ivory
and will survive underground and in the cave.
Third, I understand why you don't know this.
Angels do not look behind them
to see why they can fly.

Where we are the wind
that feeds the fish and weeps

From a poem by Ron Tanaka

Knowing Tanaka

by a vision
of standing on your mountain; I saw you

being the wind
that feeds the fish and weeps.

You were woman you were man
you were all that we dream of poets

you were the cry of young life you were
my cry you were our many cries together; your mountain

is my mountain. Our reservations are such

that you are surrounded
by earthquake and sea, I
by Navajos.

PART FIVE

AND SOME OTHERS . . .

"I come from a long line
of eloquent illiterates . . ."
—Lorna Dee Cervantes

Mission bells

"The Indians of California may be compared to a species of
monkey, for naught do they express interest, except in imi-
tating the actions of others, and particularly in copying the
ways of the 'razon' or white men, whom they respect as
being much superior to themselves."
—Fr. Geronimo Boscana, 1825

"The missions have . . . been of the highest importance to
California, and the government cannot be too careful to pro-
mote their welfare as the prosperity of the country . . . is
dependent on them."   —F. W. Beechey, 1828

We poets
have let the copal incense –
handed down
from ancient ones,
from earth-nerve singers
linking one olfactory poet
to another –
slink nearly visible
into the corners
of this room.
"It smells like a Catholic Church in here!"
says one whiteman
who has come to avoid
the native wind
rushing from our tongues
to simmer in the brown
of his beard. This is why
         we sing here
         in the Mission,
         in the barrio,
         in the sound
         of presidio bells
that are old enough
to sing lower than fire
and still ring
and swing in the air
smashing us
like so many red bugs
between the silver clapper
and the sound.

Magic Arthur

Magic Arthur
is one of those things
that become part of your life
thoroughly
so you can't imagine
the before-time
      faded into myth
      into half-evolved
      half-recalled
      memory.
The years fold up and increase
yet seem to have telescoped
single moments; time,
an immense addict for human pain,
snaps into the curve
of my soul-shaped mirrors,
sitting on the edge
of each hard sharp deadly hand
that clashes inward on my heart
like a great Iron Maiden.
It feels so good
      so good
      when the magic of love comes
      to patiently file
      the sharpness down
      into something softly newborn.
You, my magician, are
like that, sidling gently
into my life, a beautiful
sleight of hand.

Iron Maiden: Originally a torture device, a cage into which a
    person steps. When the door is closed, spikes are driven
    through one's body. In this poem, it is seen as a stage
    magician's prop, where the person inside the cage steps out
    unharmed.

The difference between us, fullblood woman, is with my ancestors, your descendants

Beat different drums,
sing different songs;
you dance round,
I dance oblong;
you intone ancient words,
I chatter aimlessly;
your cradleboard is quilled buckskin,
I have Kinsey and Pampers;
you sing and magic-talk,
I cry and confess

and so it goes
our differences dancing between us
riding double on a high white fence

sheltering mums on one side,
on the other touching yucca.

The poet as deciduous woods

for Maurice Kenny

The curled leaves, serrated,
straight, red brown green grey leaves
are dropping from my face,
a middle-aged beard unshaven,
in all the shapes, different weights,
mute in their twisted, graceful fall.

The falling flesh of trees
seeks empty places, cavities
that shape them into fossil songs
and keep their veins
glowing in the snow.

In this world
with poets as with trees
the flying and dying
of our colored leaves
is a sign
we are disappeared
into another
anonymous season.
The pruning
is posthumous
always.

For Mabel: Pomo basketmaster and doctor

Medicine song
moves air
into filaments
of skin; lets us
believe
we felt the storm
push our hands
into the redbud.
Grasses weep
upward into clouds,
grey and black
like tiny feathers,
tan and red
like baskets.
In monotone daylight
is the sound
   the sound
      of healing bone.

Donner Pass song

For a Laguna singer in Richmond

Your song
　　　　endless trees
　　　　on liquid mountains
　　　　shaping under
　　　　a moon grown fat
　　　　on warm sweet
　　　　strong summer smells,
　　　　circling like sphinx moths
　　　　and trembling
　　　　in your high distant sound,
　　　　these

Songs of
　　　　twisting our spirits
　　　　as they run and this bathing
　　　　of our bodies in mountain basalt,
　　　　ourselves singing
　　　　together, combining our bones,
　　　　content to hear
　　　　those old Laguna songs
　　　　draw the dance-time near.

Quarrel between space partners

I walked into your bedroom
bareheaded and muzzled,
armed with copper words
corroding in a shimmer
down my hands. I watched you
look up, canine, and pull
sidewise that mouth
into a foreign galaxy
await with alien women
to stretch and fold you,
eggside-first,
into a new atmosphere.

I sing the same lines to you
over and over, the notes
skidding through black vacuum
like quarterhorses, haunches under
and heads up. And you fade
cutting back to the herd
your hooves beating crescents
into the placenta of our vessel.

How many beats do I wait between words?
How many keys do I fit to the mask
till the fastener comes apart
revealing us as words at war?
We are falling, our wings
are shrieking. Your deathray snaps
like a toad's tongue at me
spinning what's left
to a cobweb sun.

Politic

I lean
on my weeping
as the years
careen by
saying as one
choking
as one removing
burrs and ticks
from her skin
"I am alone now" yet
won't forget
the years of lifetimes
so very alone
in your oak smoke scented
company.
Freeing the song
from the music
is my poet's task;
the words
must be flaked
from their matrix.
For this I was
gripped in time
like soft red clay
till I believed
in my inborn
Indian flaw
the dull and sagging
squaw
reflected from you
and settled now
on my skin
like diatoms
in earth.
And then you said
I wasn't worth it.

Reminiscence

For Brenda

Time was when the buffalo musk between us
trapped moths by its light, then released them
pollinated: we soared past mountains,
eagles aglow, stopping only to fall talon-quick
for rabbit, or clack our beaks in dialogue stolen
behind winter's back.

Time was when snow would melt for having fallen
between us   and storms were guardians
only darkness watched to extend life-giving seed
to share, knowing it a matter of time and space
that our hearts might have room for
another sky.

For Jane Penn

Morongo Indian Reservation, 1973

A very long time ago when I thought
poems weren't real, might have

passed you by and never learned
to lean on your song, mourning dissolution

of Cahuilla warsongs, having mourned
the earlessness of our one-eyed-Ford young.

The brown grass brush crackle of you
has seized my arm, pulled the hiding-hair from my eyes,

caused my ears to listen, my soul
to evaporate; made me see long, dark flickering

of ironwood Cahuilla shadows cast
growing from our spirit-reach and calling my songs

to stand
humble.

"One-eyed-Ford": Phrase from a popular 49 ("When the dance
    is over, sweetheart, let me take you home in my one-eyed
    Ford.")

PART SIX

HOPI OVERLAY: TURQUOISE WORDS
GOING HOME

"Raspberry
colored
on neatly
pruned bushes
tempting
though thorny
to fat fingers
unaccustomed
to picking
in the moonlight."
    "Poem for Wendy" by
    Maurice Kenny, 1978

Gulls on the mudflat: San Francisco Bay

To the earth brought down
onto crustacean-hunting ground.
Feathered atlatls move above earth
healing in the salt air curves,
shaping in the caves of wind.

No sound
at the barest touch
of surface slipping
along surface.
Gulls imitate rain
respond squawking
to Miwok songs,
make hunting magic
to freeze stickleback
in their tidepools,
carve trails
through ochre lichen
to catch bits of salt,
separate elements
like alchemists
grinding sand and brine
into gold and sprinkling it
with their wingtips,
sucking it up
in hooked pipette beaks
so much a part
of a single world
with the songs they bear
hungry and strong.

So intense
are their downward swings
that earth on its axis
postpones its turns
as the movement will pull,
lick and loosen
the water.

Atlatl: Spear-thrower.

94

Bird at the base of a tree

Good to be
small enough
to fit between
the tree roots,
disturb or
wedge hard
against no one.
Aging
like a
bird: graceful
        silent
        airborne

but every season making
a giant roar,
a bear-sized roar,
a year-older roar.

The man who dreamt he was turquoise

From a dream by Arthur Murata

I know the man
who was the form
of turquoise lifted
into air and the man
who knew the artist's
feel, hands that rub
shapes into the form
and surround, search
and find. I know
the man who dreamt
he was turquoise,
laid in matrix,
waiting, following
the artist, finding
the form, chiseling
the night, loving him,
holding him, feeling
of him the red fingers,
peeling of him
along shell and
layers of loam
and the pressing
pounds. I know the man
who was held and
who felt the peeling
away. I know the man
who lay in the mountain
till the artist
was born who would
chip and fit, who
would hold, who would
set the form into
sandcast silver, who
would wear the form
in proud dreams.
I know the man
who believed in the man
who would love the form,

who would direct the
forming, who would
contain the form, who
would long for the
flowing. I know the man
who knows turquoise
from inside-out,
in a wholeness, who
becomes the shape
moving through the matrix
no different from
a cradle.
I know the man
who found his years
piled up under earth
and felt the earth
shift and change
around him, who laid
with his eyes shut
waiting patiently
for the mines to be
opened. I know the man
who knows the artist
and changes his color
at will, touched
and found between
blue and brown.
I know the man
whose fingers bleed
tearing up through
earth; I know the man
who built his strength
bringing turquoise
to the sky. He told me
stones are like this:
bones wrapped in heat
and hardness, rasping
the seasons around
on a gourd and
holding the planet
in place.

Chicago

is a mystery to me
for it does not extend
beyond the foodless corridors
of O'Hare Airport yet
does bring out
the foreigner in me
feeling her way
along the ground
touching ice and earth,
determining existence,
and mapping a path
from west to east
and back again.

All the many things
I've heard about Chicago
narrow into the frame
of this hour: yellow light
slanting across the smoke,
hands groping
toward what is hoped
is a coffee pot,
lights whirling
and spinning the planes to earth,
alien promises
served on toothpicks
in the cocktails,
Ojibwa songs
from behind the jukebox.

The parts of a poet

for Terry Garey

Loving

the pottery goodness
of my body

> settled down on flowers,
> pulling pollen in great
> handfuls; full & ready
>
> parts of me are pinned
> to earth, parts of me
> undermine song, parts
> of me spread on the water,
> parts of me form a rainbow
> bridge, parts of me follow
> the sandfish, parts of me
> are a woman who judges.

Mount Saint Helens: An Indian woman's song

March 30, 1980

Having unbuckled themselves
from their airline seats
the passengers found each
a tiny window on the left side
of the jet and stared like voyeurs
into the bellows of her throat,
watched the convulsions shaking her
till she raged
and waved her round hands
in the sky.

Some gave up easily,
said "She looks just like
any mountain covered with snow
as winter eases
into spring." Others
closed their eyes,
and waited for supper.
I applauded,
called for an encore,
and wished to soar
around her in an honoring dance
because in her labor
she holds
the planet in place.

In five minutes
we had flown completely by,
leaving her eastern slope blackened
and eyelids fluttering
as one slowly waking.

Southeast
Mazama nods
and waits.

Mazama: The huge volcano in Oregon whose eruption created
    Crater Lake. From an airplane at 35,000 feet, Mount St.
    Helens and Crater Lake may be seen at roughly the same
    time.

100

Directions for the strategic hunter

You: screening me
with your eyes,
Strategic Hunter,
you have caught me
hooves swollen
in snowcrust,
antlers knotted
by leafless wind.

You: playing no games
with my body now.

To hunt me down
you have to be firm
in every nerve
that touches earth;
you have
to recall
the pollen;
you have
to grow velvet horns;
you must sink
into you and
then, covered with tundra,
out.

The loving of a quiet image

for Arthur Murata

The loving of a quiet image

(turning around and around till
it turns into a man) and then
manlike, more magic than man,
it's a bear or a lion or
a gazelle . . . . Quiet

in ways that are real, ways
that like dust surround my feet
with ancient sand so that I stand
with toes afraid to move

because something will shift,
will change, will go away.
Imagine a mountain
so tall and silent that even
to hiss in a whisper
the word "love" will make

the mountain lie back and melt
as one who has surfaced on the sun
and seen too much
of nearly everything.

Remembering a Catholic girlhood in El Cerrito

At dawn the church was full of us kids
who were told to pray but instead removed
rosaries with clicks & clacks from their snap-boxes
& squeezed them till the beads burst
like our own caged thoughts; they were tangible
hard things between our fingers,
the prayers you could feel, eager
to slip & shudder from one another,
taking on the soft bones of the fingers
that held them, unstrung yet
tied to this planet like teeth.

Dusted with incense
we would move our heads downward
eyes cornered so the Sisters couldn't see
how we copied the almost-women
with color on our lips.

A sort of logic: The stroke

For Grandma

The sea's logic: a crush,
the shore eaten. Mussels
separate from stone,
anemone is bruised; salt air
is singled out and severed
from the sand.
The wolf tooth: sings
through the rabbit,
red on grey fur and steam
on the snow.
Loosened leaves: browned
gathered as they float
from groves of aspen,
freed to fall on the earth
to feed searching for a teat.
Star blizzard logic: suns shrink
so small as to blink out finally,
to nova, to flash and snap
spreading lightyears out.
The massive yawn and stretch
of thunder: the stillness
following, the eyes closed,
luminescence rescinded.
Rain: lashing, kissing,
displacing, swelling, restoring,
receding. Death logic,
sequence of death before death:
Pauline in the dark.
Let loose my hand
that strains toward earth
as you slip, still talking,
to the sky. This is gentle,
irresistible, logical.

Summer evenings in Tucson remembered

Flower winds
whirl and lap
against my eyes;
fat ladies
pat their hands
plumply
on my face.

From adobe earth ovens
full of bread,
finished and brown
and round like turtles,
the summer sweetness
soaks the air.

Dreaming from the fingers

Another one of those dreams
where I grind my own colors
& bite the basket of this world
inserting filed teeth
between warp & weft
to lift the twining round its rods
& pull it apart; undoing my baskets
I take the old bent grasses
& put them to soak, let the reeds
stretch straight again & weave
my wet skin in with them,
twining moons & arrows into dark designs.
Under my hand is ground
the green mold, the black earth,
the little last touches; up & down
obliquely my fingers wink in the air,
stroking the long reeds with water,
pulling about the dust caught
floating by the first slight circles
of sunrise.

Old-time potter

So cautious my art
is become: spinning its career
hung between that world
and that world. And this morning
I'm gone for clay
to wrap around cactus
and bear that impression
of bird's feet and spines,
to mix them together,
to grind my bones
indistinguished from stones
and fire them
under potsherds and dung
to swallow them
into my lungs
and pull them from the oven
fully formed but stillborn.

Magic marker: Creation story

I speak
from a place
of charmed air; my bones are structure

of stone
and stand profiled
against the eve of extinction.

I am the last beast
of one particular variety.
I am a mutation from many tongues.

My poems are water
seeping onto this world
from space; I befuddle the Twin Poles

who stabilize too much
this world in its burning. Let it turn
just sudden enough

to render feather into steel
and feel its breath
freeze into a god.

East Coast city scene: Connecticut

In a rust-sprinkled roll
the "El" grumbles
over watchful horses
pried from concrete and iron
made head-down to graze the pavement
splitting the ice
with hollow hooves.

On their palomino backs
red letters spell "This
is where you land
when you fall from the sky,
when your search carries you east
and your coffee
is cold."

Now that I know these things
I will not consult
the guidebook again.

Water colors

My painted people are orphans; they take me
to earth in great strides and beg the rain;

they are not afraid to strike the sun nor
open the water that seals their throats;

they are rich with pottery dust on their hands,
they are big with the pregnancy of peace;

they shoulder my brushes as I draw them dancing,
they call me mama, they call me orphan.

Poet Woman's mitosis: Dividing all the cells apart

> "It is a little unfair to the Indian that we expect
> him to make a permanent transition from a
> primitive to an ultra-modern citizen overnight —
> a feat which took us thousands of years to ac-
> complish . . ."—J. Poncel, Tucson Indian
> School, 1950

Urban Halfbreed, burro-faced
no more nor less than the number
of remembered songs and the learning
to sing them a new way.
The Singers are of another generation;
throats ready with the bell and beat of the sky
while mine can do no more than mimic
the sound heard while my hand danced on paper
looking for the rattle of old words.
Here I am now: body and heart and soul Hopi,
details, pinpoints, tongue something else,
foreign and familiar at once
like sores that grow and burst
no matter what.

Going in and out of fashion

Going in
and out
of fashion

must be accepted
like gypsy moths
in the trees;

weather changes,
poles
reverse;

pullings, moldings
that shape
history

must pull and mold
without
letting up

for even
one second.
No one

must be let
to rest.
The whole climate

rushes into change.
Last year
they listened

to my long-caught
native songs;
this year they

purge themselves
with some
other

broken tongue.
They search
in this world

for someone
they haven't damaged;
each of us

in turn
is seen
and forgotten.

November: San Joaquin Valley

Tumbleweed sticks to the stunned
and stripped valley
recalling the drought or the day
we turned the wind around
and slept dreamless one year
only to dream too much the year following.
Field after field there are invisible mountains
beyond the cotton baled into tightly bound trucks;
the white mounds mark the boundaries of farms
like nations backed up against each other
forever on the brink of war.
Red-winged blackbirds and magpies
lean anchored to the barbed wire,
stiffly move in the stillness.
Peach trees have slimmed and dropped their leaves,
hardening brown for winter
and stretching their hands
between the smudge pots.

I run the length of this valley
flatfooted into its visions

with eyes closed tight
on the western horizon,

white with fatigue,
holding my breath, remaining deaf.

Like infants dressed in baptismal robes
I gather the dreams back to me in this place

and promise again
to protect what's left.

Hopi overlay: Turquoise words going home

Falling through the years
like dandelion dust or turquoise
chipped from the matrix and flying,
I am set in troubled silver.
I know there's a first time
for everything, even closed words,
even a finishing. My songs seem undone
when they stompdance naked in the moonlight
but children peeping from under dark porches
laugh all the ups and downs in together.

I'll take my old age early
and watch them play my poems
into cat's-cradles.

PART SEVEN

BUILDER KACHINA: HOME-GOING

A journey from my mother's
land to my father's land,
August, 1977

1. Highway 5: The journey begins

San Joaquin Valley, California

Does it tickle? going down
on the right side of your spine
like this?   Your hair
is drought-bobbed; can't see the
lean grass blow ripple on ripple
as in years before. And where
are the mustard flowers?

> Like ringworm: a golfcourse
> posted to the topography
> there   where being dry
> is a way of being in pain.
>
> The tumbleweed stays green.
> It plays, like Coyote,
> with our senses: dries up,
> blows away when it rains.
> Tumbleweed blowing about
> with strength in the stretching
> of the roots.

Cabbage-butterflies
on the windshield: papery-yellow,
successful suicides.
"Lots of leaves" says Arthur.

2. Entering the desert: Big circles running

Mojave Desert, California

Mounting the Tehachapis
where my magic is mapped
in desert pulse: Hopi-style,
I wrap the wind about my legs
and cuff my wrists in cactus flowers.
Just over the mountain, then east
through blowing sand, then a leap
over the river, and almost home.

All this is a part of my soul's fossil strata:
where the shock of English fog
tornados with the mammoth bones
in my blood.

> Skin within the setting sun,
> the sun itself
> setting into Hopi clay;
> the clay at my feet
> that was a butte or mountain
> or something that
> approached the sky.
> Using my eyes to see distance
> not words in print.
> The strength is of earth
> not the being on earth.

Arthur and I like aliens,
like space dust, like
San Francisco Bay Area beach debris.
We are unseen explorers
reaching for a morning to which
we are tied.
We'll roll to the river,
to the slope of the world's rim
where California gives up and
Arizona begins. This traveling
is the wait between dimensions;
someone
is
expecting
us.

Earth airborne, dust
in the wind: ourselves
carried into the sky
on the backs of bees
pollinating with poems.

Tehachapis: A mountain range in California, separating the
    northern agricultural valleys from the southern deserts.

3. Chipped from the Cliff: Anasazi Traveler

Verde Valley, Phoenix, & Flagstaff, Arizona

Going east at Kingman
strata are layered
for fossils to sleep inside
encased and safe.
Going south: Mogollon Rim
and all that – the earth
is getting older.
On our backs inside California
we fail to notice this:
in the rolling brown flesh mounds
of the coast we don't see
the hollowing, the thinning,
the leaning, the honeycombing.
Only bones remain
for our touch, our memory,
our departing. This is where
the Hopi have prayed
to keep the blood flowing
though it flows on bare bones
through the earth beating
in sheets of water.

Transformed into mesas,
the ancient mountains
are museum monuments
to the animal flesh of earth
they once were . . . the white man
sucks their marrow and
throws them down without
a thought.

Mogollon Rim: A geological feature in Arizona, north of
Phoenix.

The rain greets us
like old friends.
In California
the deadly silent missions
drove the rain away.

All the land
is looking up!
Like smoky quartz
the sky is singing!
All the land
is looking up!
The land
is listening,
the hands
are raised up!
Cicadas graze
in pockets of moisture;
the rain comes,
fills up the mouth
open beneath.

Phoenix. City lights
an ungiving poison.
Alien sounds
on my back pound
and shake the streets.
But the songs flow!
Through copper and lead
radiated water, overcleaned,
careens in an underground
mess of pipes. Singing for
the deaf, songs I hear
alone. Songs that trail me
out of the city.

Up the rim one lone pine tree
among aspens – hunkered and timid,
blanket-wrapped old Indian.
A maverick like me, there standing
against the mountain
a single pine
in a time
of its own.

My soul is running away
on these mountains. I try
to identify the rigid pole
inside my breast: an approach
of dignity? The tearing of my soul
about thunderheads or my words
into rain? The scattering of
my smallest bones on the rocks?
The touch of dormant volcanoes,
the scars of old eruptions?

> Metal scales bouncing from the sun
> a long-nosed lizard does not run but stays
> to welcome this Hopi home to the heart.
> Montezuma's Castle: way up out of the
>   reach
> of tourists the stones cling, bake
> into each other, struggle and win,
> remain alive. The tourists move them
> four inches a year,
> the seismologist says.   Fault creep.

Montezuma's Castle: A prehistoric ruin north of Phoenix; not
    related in any way to Montezuma.

After all this
we're still
escaping the drought.
Homes change, roads
wash out.
Dryness is a seasonal thing
marked in centuries
not in sleeps; the weather
is not homeless.
Here is where I remember:
I am Anasazi, ancient
cliff-dweller, thing
that has stuck
on the face of the world
all this time.

Nothing of great value here.
Just my story. A halfbreed goes
from one half-home to the other;
strings of half-homes
all over the world.
Each one is a sound
that shakes the strength
of silence.
Solution: let the thunder
roll me north! Let me climb,
each word a foothold, into
Kachina Home! Let me find
the Cloud People!

Anasazi: A Navajo word meaning "The Ancient Ones," the
cliff-dwelling ancestors of the Hopi and other Pueblo
people.

4. Builder Kachina: Home-going

Third Mesa, Hopi Reservation, Arizona

Thirty years ago
a shred of brown cotton blew
from the cottonwoods
of Hotevilla; the sky lightened
to give it a passing to the west.
I remember: one lone Hopi
made it to the sea. It was 1947
but the scars are fresh
in me. They speak in my flesh,
they rasp and shake in my bones,
they circle like buzzards
in my soul.

Must I explain why
the songs are stiff and shy?
Like this: too much voice
about me already
to shuffle in with
my tuneless noise.
California moves my pen
but Hotevilla dashes through my blood
like a great and
crazy dragonfly.

Hotevilla: A Hopi village on the westernmost mesa.

Carefully
the way we plant the corn
in single places, each place
a hole just one finger around.
We'll build your roots
that way. He said this
as badgers marked their
parallel lines on his skin,
each one a clan mark,
as Builder Kachina
hooted beside him, invisible
yet touching me all over
with his sound.
What we can't find
we'll build but
slowly,
slowly.

Builder Kachina: The identities and roles of the Kachina Holy
    People are traditionally somewhat flexible; this is one that
    is not part of the Hopi tradition, but is part of my
    imagination.

Epilog

Drop a kernel of corn on a rock
and say a prayer. It will shoot up
proud and green, tassel out,
pull the next crop from the thunderheads.
That's the Hopi way.
If the corn doesn't grow
you eat the rocks,
drink the clouds
on the distant plains.

Silko and Allen and Harjo and me:
our teeth are hard
from the rocks we eat.

Leslie Silko, Paula Gunn Allen, Joy Harjo: Modern Indian
   women writers.

Designed by William Bright

Set in Oracle type by
Freedmens' Organization
Los Angeles

Printed by BookCrafters
Chelsea, Michigan

Malki Museum Press
Morongo Indian Reservation